by
Thomas
Kingsley
Troupe

illustrated by
D.C. Ice

PICTURE WINDOW BOOKS
a capstone imprint

The Legend of the
Werewolf

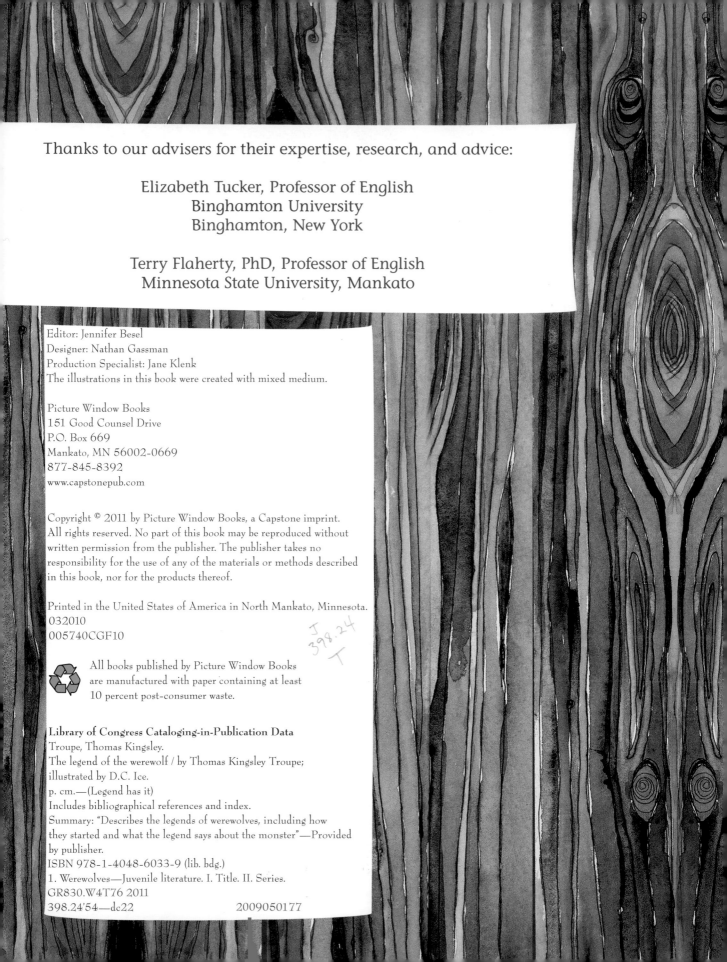

Thanks to our advisers for their expertise, research, and advice:

Elizabeth Tucker, Professor of English
Binghamton University
Binghamton, New York

Terry Flaherty, PhD, Professor of English
Minnesota State University, Mankato

Editor: Jennifer Besel
Designer: Nathan Gassman
Production Specialist: Jane Klenk
The illustrations in this book were created with mixed medium.

Picture Window Books
151 Good Counsel Drive
P.O. Box 669
Mankato, MN 56002-0669
877-845-8392
www.capstonepub.com

Printed in the United States of America in North Mankato, Minnesota.
032010
005740CGF10

J
398.24
T

All books published by Picture Window Books
are manufactured with paper containing at least
10 percent post-consumer waste.

Library of Congress Cataloging-in-Publication Data
Troupe, Thomas Kingsley.
The legend of the werewolf / by Thomas Kingsley Troupe;
illustrated by D.C. Ice.
p. cm.—(Legend has it)
Includes bibliographical references and index.
Summary: "Describes the legends of werewolves, including how
they started and what the legend says about the monster"—Provided
by publisher.
ISBN 978-1-4048-6033-9 (lib. bdg.)
1. Werewolves—Juvenile literature. I. Title. II. Series.
GR830.W4T76 2011
398.24'54—dc22   2009050177

TABLE of CONTENTS

WEREWOLF on the LOOSE

The moon is full and bright. In the distance a creature howls. The werewolf is on the loose!

The werewolf legends we know today started hundreds of years ago in Europe. In the tales, werewolves are people who change into terrible beasts. They hunt and kill anything.

During the Middle Ages, there were terrible killings. Victims were found with bite marks and bloody slashes. No one wanted to believe humans would do such things.

Stories of people who turn into werewolves were used to explain the murders.

As the stories spread, people became
afraid for their lives. They tried to spot anyone
with werewolf traits. They thought people with
eyebrows that grew close together were werewolves.
People with long fingernails were werewolves too.

8

Stories said that if a wolfsbane flower cast a yellow shadow on someone's chin, that person was a werewolf.

A SCARY SIGHT

How does a person become a werewolf?
Some stories say that a werewolf bite
brings a **terrible curse.**
Once the bite heals, the victim
becomes a werewolf too.

Other stories say sleeping
beneath a full moon causes
people to become werewolves.

People with the curse change into werewolves under a full moon. They run through the moonlight to hunt prey.

Before the sun comes up, they become human again.

They can't remember what they did as werewolves.

CREATURE FEATURES

With their eyes and ears, werewolves can see and hear better than any human.

Long, pointy fangs are perfect for tearing apart food.

Long, thick hair covers their bodies, keeping the creatures warm on dark nights.

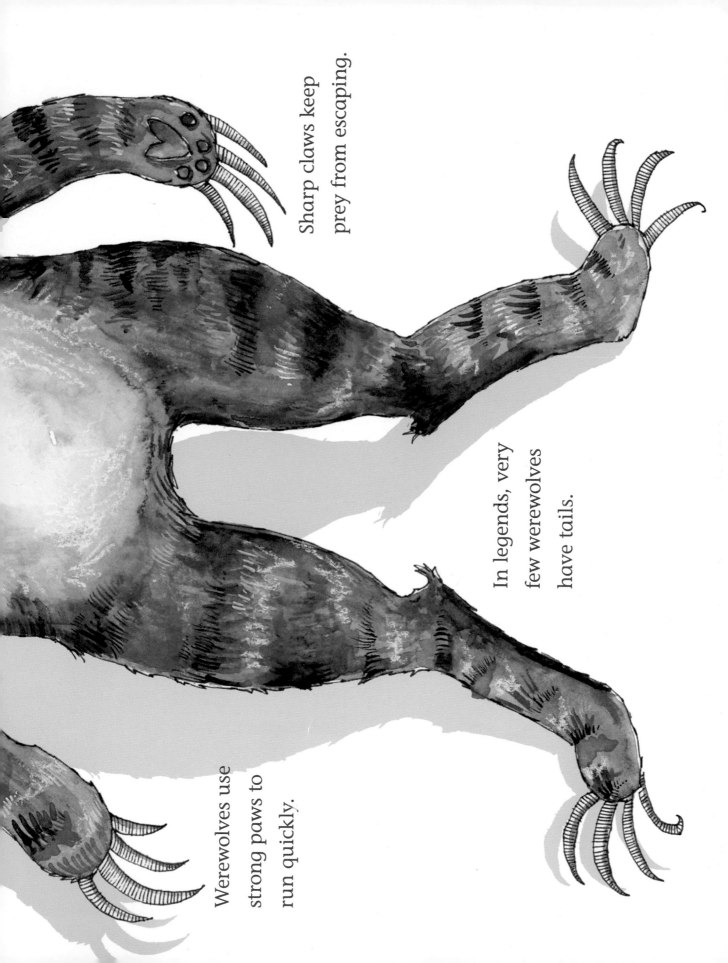

Sharp claws keep prey from escaping.

In legends, very few werewolves have tails.

Werewolves use strong paws to run quickly.

The change from person to werewolf is
thought to be very painful. Bones twist
and muscles stretch. Even thick hair
growing through the skin hurts.

The change makes the creature

very angry and hungry!

The werewolf is ready to hunt.

WEREWOLF POWERS

According to legend, werewolves have incredible strength. They can rip through trees and fences.

They are very hard to fight off.

Werewolves have super senses.

They can spot victims from far away, even in the dark of night. They can smell prey for miles. These monsters can hear better than a normal wolf.

If a werewolf wants to find something to eat ... **it will.**

STOPPING a WEREWOLF

A silver bullet is the best way to destroy a werewolf. Legends say werewolves can't stand silver. A silver bullet to a werewolf's heart will kill the creature instantly.

Don't have a silver bullet? Some believed saying the wolf's human name would turn it back to normal. That is, of course, if you knew the werewolf's name!

Jasper

Betty

Olivia

Travis

Will

WEREWOLVES of the WORLD

Werewolf legends have scared people around the world. In Poland, some people feared birthmarks. Stories said a baby born with a birthmark could be a werewolf.

In Argentina, a family didn't want to have
seven sons in a row. Stories said the seventh
son would turn into a werewolf.

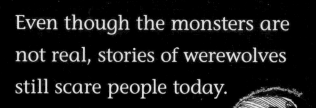

Even though the monsters are not real, stories of werewolves still scare people today.

Hear that howl in the night?

It's just a dog baying at the moon ... **or is it?**

GLOSSARY

birthmark—a mark on a person's skin that has been there since birth

curse—an evil spell

legend—a story handed down from earlier times that could seem believable

Middle Ages—a period of time between the years 500 and 1500

prey—an animal hunted by another animal for food

trait—a quality that makes one thing different from another

victim—a person who is hurt, killed, or made to suffer

READ MORE

Pipe, Jim. *Werewolves*. Tales of Horror. New York: Bearport Pub., 2007.

Sautter, Aaron. *Werewolves*. Monsters. Mankato, Minn.: Capstone Press, 2007.

Townsend, John. *Werewolf Attack*. Crabtree Contact. New York: Crabtree Pub. Co., 2009.

Whiting, Jim. *Scary Monsters*. Really Scary Stuff. Mankato, Minn.: Capstone Press, 2010.

OOOOOO   Oww Oww OOOOOOOOOO

INTERNET SITES

FactHound offers a safe, fun way to find Internet sites related to this book. All of the sites on FactHound have been researched by our staff.

Here's all you do:

Visit *www.facthound.com*

FactHound will fetch the best sites for you!

INDEX

LEGEND HAS IT
OTHER TITLES

**The Legend of
the Bermuda Triangle**

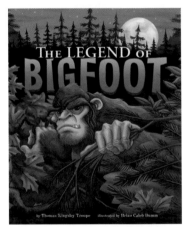

The Legend of Bigfoot

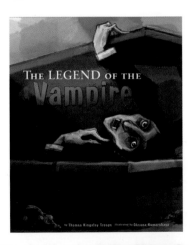

The Legend of the Vampire